The Bhagavad Gita

Song of God

Bhagavad Gita

Copyright 2012
All rights reserved

ISBN 978-0-9682461-3-9

Preface

For over 2,000 years, the *Bhagavad Gita* has been a great source of inspiration to Hindus, as well as both eastern and western seekers of wisdom. Like many great thinkers such as Albert Einstein, Mahatma Gandhi, Ralph Waldo Emerson, Henry David Thoreau, and T.S. Eliot, who were enthused by the Gita, I too am inspired by its profound wisdom. As a mortal being, I consider myself fortunate to have read the *Bhagavad Gita*, for if I had died without reading it, I would have missed this precious knowledge that is so thoughtful and worthy of reverence.

In this book, I have tried my utmost to keep the dialogue between Krishna and Arjuna simple. The insertion of words in parentheses in various parts of the text is merely to give a clearer understanding of some verses. It is possible that when analyzing the Gita, many will come to their own conclusions, depending on their interpretation of some of the teachings. With this in mind, it is highly unlikely to find a single translation of the Gita that satisfies every person. For those seeking an in-depth analysis or commentaries on the Gita, I suggest that readers take a look at a number of scholarly translations of the Gita.

Looking back over the years, I recall meeting an elderly gentleman who took me by surprise when he asked if I knew how to die. As I stood silent and somewhat puzzled by his question, he gently smiled and said that the most important thing for us to remember when dying is to silently utter the sacred syllable OM and to focus our thoughts on God with love in our hearts, for in doing so one could take refuge in the Supreme (Brahman). What caught my attention was his calmly saying that after he dies, he will not go to a hell to be punished; instead, through the cycle of birth, death and rebirth, he will be given a series of chances to strive for self-discipline. So while we are alive, we have the opportunity to do as much good as we want to for the betterment of humanity and for our own self-improvement.

Some terms used in the Gita:
Ahamkara: "I-maker," egoism, individuality
Ahimsa: non-violence
Atman: soul, self, spirit
Bhagavad Gita: Song of God
Bhakti: loving devotion
Brahman: the Absolute, the Ultimate Reality, the All-Pervading Lord
Buddhi: intellect, reason, wisdom, understanding, intelligence
Dharma: law, righteousness, sacred duty, order
Gunas: qualities, constituents: refers to the three qualities of nature: sattva, rajas and tamas
Guru: spiritual teacher
Jiva: individual soul
Jnana: knowledge, wisdom
Kala: time
Kama: desire, pleasure
Karma: action, work, deed
Manas: mind
Maya: illusion, illusive power
Moha: delusion, bewilderment
Moksha: liberation, freedom, release
OM: the sound-symbol for the Absolute Reality, a sacred syllable; denotes God.
Paramatman: the Supreme Soul
Phala: the fruit, the results of one's actions
Prakriti: nature, matter
Prana: life-breath, vital energy, vital air
Purusha: spirit, the living entity
Purushottama: the Supreme Spirit, Supreme Being
Samadhi: (deep) concentration
Samsara: the cycle of birth, death, and rebirth
Sankhya: one of the many branches of Hindu philosophy
Sannyasa: renunciation

Shanti: peace
Shraddha: faith
Sukha: joy, happiness
Tapas: austerity, penance
Tyaga: relinquishment, abandonment; giving up the fruits of one's action
Veda(s): "knowledge," scriptures comprising of the Rig-veda, Yajur-veda, Sama-veda and Atharva-veda
Yajna: sacrifice, worship, offering
Yoga: discipline, union with God, self-discipline

INTRODUCTION

The Bhagavad Gita is a small part of the famous Hindu epic, the *Mahabharata*, which revolves around the dispute between two sets of cousins regarding the succession to an ancient kingdom. These cousins were the sons of two royal brothers named Pandu and Dhritarashtra. Because Dhritarashtra was born blind, his younger brother Pandu became the ruler. Sadly, after ruling for quite some time, Pandu passed away, and Dhritarashtra assumed the throne. Pandu's five young sons, called the Pandavas, were then brought to Dhritarashtra's court to be taken care of along with their cousins, called the Kauravas, who were the sons of the blind king Dhritarashtra.

In the course of time the Pandava brothers became admirable in warfare. One of the Pandavas, Arjuna, grew to become an accomplished pupil of a military instructor named Drona, who taught him the art of warfare.

Soon, the eldest son of Dhritarashtra, Duryodhana, grew jealous of the Pandavas, who were virtuous and who excelled in their skills. When the eldest of the Pandavas, Yudhishthira, was declared the rightful heir to the throne, Duryodhana grew even more jealous and began thinking of ways to get rid of the Pandavas, so that he could become the ruler. A cunning uncle named Shakuni then encouraged the envious Duryodhana to invite Yudhishthira, who was fond of gambling, to play dice games. Unfortunately, Yudhishthira kept losing to the point where he even put his kingdom at stake. Sadly, he lost everything and was sent into exile along with his brothers for thirteen years.

After their term in exile ended, the Pandavas returned to claim their rightful share of the kingdom, but Duryodhana vehemently refused, making war inevitable. In spite of all efforts to avert war by other relatives through peace talks, no one could persuade the stubborn Duryodhana.

Both Arjuna and Duryodhana then set off to meet with Krishna, who had ties with both sets of cousins, to seek his support in war. At this meeting, Krishna declared that he would not fight and gave them the choice of either having him alone or his large army for support. Arjuna chose Krishna to be his charioteer while the proud Duryodhana got Krishna's large army.

The forces of both armies then gathered to fight on the battlefield of Kurukshetra, thus making this the setting of the *Bhagavad Gita*, commonly called the *Song of God*. This famous battle to uphold righteousness and prevent disorder lasted eighteen days, ending with the victory of the Pandavas.

The Bhagavad Gita begins with the blind king Dhritarashtra, who wishes to hear an account of the war, asking his minister Sanjaya to tell him what his sons and the sons of his brother Pandu did when they gathered on the battlefield of Kurukshetra. Following this, the names of many great heroes, archers and brave kings are mentioned, as well as the thunderous sounds of conches, drums, cymbals, and horns.

On the battlefield, Arjuna asks his charioteer Krishna to position his chariot between the two armies. As Arjuna surveys the battlefield, he becomes deeply saddened, seeing that those he is about to fight against are his own relatives and friends. Filled with pity, he lays down his bow and arrows, claiming he cannot fight against his own people. At this point, Krishna gradually replaces his uncertainty with divine knowledge, during which Arjuna comes to fully realize that Krishna is no ordinary person but an incarnation of God.

CHAPTER 1

Arjuna's Loss of Hope

1.1. **Dhritarashtra** (the blind king) **said:** O Sanjaya! Tell me what happened when my sons and the sons of Pandu met on the sacred field of Kurukshetra, eager to fight.

1.2. **Sanjaya** (the reporter) **said:** Seeing the army of the Pandavas assembled for battle, your son Duryodhana approached his teacher Drona and said:

1.3. O respected teacher, look at the great Pandava army assembled for battle by your talented student, the son of Drupada.

1.4. Here are great archers, brave men who are equal in warfare to Bhima and Arjuna: Yuyudhana, Virata, and the great warrior Drupada.

1.5. Also, there are heroic fighters like Dhrishtaketu, Chekitana, and the brave king of Kashi, as well as Purujit, Kuntibhoja, and Shaibya, valiant among men.

1.6. Here also are the bold Yudhamanyu, the mighty Uttamaujas, Subhadra's son, and the sons of Draupadi. They are all great warriors.

1.7. O revered priest, now let me inform you about the great chiefs on our side. I will tell you their names.

1.8. They are yourself, Bhishma, Karna, and the victorious Kripa, and also Ashvatthaman, Vikarna, and the son of Somadatta.

1.9. There are many other courageous men, who are willing to give up their lives for my sake. They bear various weapons and are skilled in warfare.

1.10. The strength of our army protected by Bhishma is enormous, but the strength of the Pandavas (army) protected by Bhima is limited.

1.11. So, as all of you stand positioned in your appropriate places, you must protect Bhishma on all sides.

1.12. After this, the mighty Bhishma, the valiant elder of the Kurus, roared like a lion and blew his conch loudly, giving joy to Duryodhana.

1.13. Following that, conches, kettledrums, horns, cymbals and drums blared aloud, causing a tumultuous sound.

1.14. Then, standing in their grand chariot drawn by white horses, Krishna and Arjuna blew their divine conches.

1.15. Krishna blew his conch called Panchajanya, Arjuna blew his conch Devadatta, and the fierce Bhima blew his great conch Paundra.

1.16-18. King Yudhishthira, the son of Kunti, blew his conch called Anantavijaya, while Nakula and Sahadeva blew their conches Sughosha and Manipushpaka. The king of Kashi, a great archer, Shikhandin the great fighter, Dhrishtadyumna, Virata, and the unconquered Satyaki, Drupada, the sons of Draupadi, as well as the strong-armed son of Subhadra, all blew their conches.

1.19. This thunderous sound tore the hearts of Dhritarashtra's sons, echoing through the sky and earth.

1.20. Then Arjuna, whose war flag bore the figure of an ape, upon seeing the sons of Dhritarashtra arrayed as the battle was about to begin, lifted up his bow.

1.21-23. Arjuna then said to his charioteer: "O Krishna, position my chariot between the two armies, for me to see those who are arrayed and with whom I must engage in this war. Let me look at those assembled here, who are eager to fight and willing to serve the evil-minded son of Dhritarashtra."

1.24-25. After being addressed by Arjuna, Krishna positioned the grand chariot between the two armies, in front of Bhishma, Drona, and all those kings, and said, "O Arjuna, look at these Kuru men assembled (for battle)!"

1.26-27. Arjuna saw in both armies: fathers, grandfathers, teachers, uncles, brothers, sons, grandsons, fathers-in-law, and friends. Upon seeing all these relatives assembled, Arjuna became filled with sadness and uttered these words:

1.28-29. **Arjuna said:** O Krishna, seeing my own relatives eager for war, I feel my limbs sink, my mouth becomes dry, my body trembles, and the hairs rise on my body.

1.30. My bow (Gandiva) slips from my hand, my skin burns. I cannot stand steady, and my mind is reeling.

1.31-34. O Krishna, I see evil signs. I do not see any good coming from killing my own relatives in battle. I do not crave for victory, nor kingdom, nor pleasures. O Krishna, of what use is kingdom, or pleasure, or even life to us? Those for whose sake we desire these things are assembled here for battle, abandoning their lives and riches. They are teachers, fathers, sons, grandfathers, uncles, grandsons, fathers-in-law, brothers-in-law, and other relations.

1.35. I do not wish to kill them, even if they slay me, O Krishna, not even for the sovereignty of the three worlds (upper, middle, and lower regions), much less for (a kingdom on) this earth.

1.36. O Krishna, What pleasure is there for us from killing these sons of Dhritarashtra? Sin will attach to us if we slay these evildoers.

1.37. Hence, we should not kill our relatives, these sons of Dhritarashtra. O Krishna, how could we be happy by slaying our own people?

1.38-39. O Krishna, even if they, with their minds overpowered by greed, do not see the evil in destroying the family and the sin in betraying friends, how could we not wish to avoid this evil, when we see the sin of destroying the family, O Krishna?

1.40. When the family is ruined, ancient family (traditional) laws are lost, and with the loss of laws, unruliness overcomes the whole family.

1.41. O Krishna, when lawlessness takes over, the women of the family become corrupted, and when women are corrupted, disorder arises in the (four) classes of society.

1.42. Such disorder leads the family to hell, as well as those who have destroyed the family, since their ancestors fall (no longer honored) when the (ritual) offerings of rice and water are lacking.

1.43. Because of the evil deeds of those who destroy the family and cause disorder in society, the ongoing family (traditional) laws are destroyed.

1.44. O Krishna, we have heard that a place in hell is sure for those whose family laws have been destroyed.

1.45. Oh, how sad! What great sin we are about to commit in wanting to kill our own relatives because of greed for the pleasures of kingship.

1.46. It would be better for me if Dhritarashtra's armed sons were to slay me in battle, while I am unarmed and offer no resistance.

1.47. **Sanjaya** (the reporter) **said:** After saying these words on the battlefield, Arjuna laid down his bow and arrows, and sank into his chariot, overwhelmed with grief.

CHAPTER 2

Philosophy and Discipline

2.1. **Sanjaya** (the reporter) **said:** Seeing Arjuna so dejected, overwhelmed with pity, and his eyes filled with tears, Krishna responded:

2.2. **Lord Krishna said:** Arjuna, how has this loss of hope come upon you at this hour of crisis? This is improper for a noble (Aryan). It is dishonorable, and does not lead to heaven.

2.3. O Arjuna, do not yield to this faintheartedness, because it is unworthy of you! Give up this cowardice and rise up (to fight)!

2.4. **Arjuna said:** O Krishna, how can I fight against Bhishma and Drona with arrows when they are worthy of respect?

2.5. It is better to live by begging for food in this world than to kill such noble teachers, since by killing these teachers, who long for wealth, all that I enjoy will be smeared with blood.

2.6. We cannot tell which is better for us, whether we should defeat them or whether they should defeat us. By killing the sons of Dhritarashtra, who are now standing before us, we would have no desire to live.

2.7. My being has been stricken by the weakness of pity. I am confused about my duty (dharma). I ask You to tell me with certainty which would be better (for me). I am Your student. Instruct me!

2.8. I cannot imagine anything that would remove my grief, which is drying up my senses, even if I were to obtain an unrivaled and prosperous kingdom on earth or even lordship over the gods.

2.9. **Sanjaya** (the reporter) **said:** Having told this to Krishna, Arjuna said, "I will not fight!" and then became silent.

2.10. As Arjuna sat dejected between the two armies, Lord Krishna, gently smiling, said these words to him:

2.11. **The Lord said:** While you speak so wisely, you grieve over those you ought not to grieve for. Those who are (truly) wise grieve neither for the living nor for the dead.

2.12. There was never a time when I did not exist, nor you, nor these kings, and never will all of us cease to exist hereafter.

2.13. Just as the soul (atman) within this body passes through childhood to youth and to old age, so the soul (after leaving the body at death) enters into another body. The wise are not bewildered about this.

2.14. Contacts with matter give rise to (feelings of) heat and cold, pleasure and pain. They are temporary (experiences), for they come and go. So endure them, O Arjuna.

2.15. O Arjuna, one who is wise and is not disturbed by these things, and to whom joy and sorrow are the same, that person is fit for immortality.

2.16. The non-existent cannot come into existence, and the existent never ceases to exist. The reality of both is perceived by the seers of truth.

2.17. Know that (Spirit) which pervades all is indestructible, and no one can destroy this imperishable Spirit.

2.18. It is (just) these bodies of the eternal embodied soul (the true self), which is imperishable and incomprehensible, that perishes. So, Arjuna, fight!

2.19. One who believes that the soul is a killer, and one who thinks it is killed, both of them do not understand that it neither kills nor is it killed.

2.20. The soul is not born, nor does it ever die, nor having been before, will it cease to be. It is never killed when the body is killed, for it is birthless, eternal, everlasting, and primeval.

2.21. Arjuna, how can one who knows the soul to be indestructible, enduring, unborn and unchanging kill anyone or cause another to kill?

2.22. Just as a person casts off worn-out clothes to put on new ones, so the embodied soul casts off worn-out bodies to enter new ones.

2.23. The soul cannot be cut by any weapon, fire cannot burn it, water cannot wet it, and it cannot be dried by the wind.

2.24. The soul cannot be severed, burned, wetted, nor dried. It is eternal, all-pervading, unchanging, immovable and everlasting.

2.25. The soul is said to be unmanifest (invisible), inconceivable, and unchanging. Hence, knowing this to be so, you should not grieve!

2.26. If you think that the soul is repeatedly born and repeatedly dies, O Arjuna, still you should not lament!

2.27. For anyone born, death is certain, and birth is certain for anyone who has passed away. Hence, you should not lament over what is inescapable.

2.28. O Arjuna, all beings (before birth) are unmanifest in the beginning, they are manifest (visible) in the middle (between birth and death), and are unmanifest again in the end (after death). Therefore, why do you lament?

2.29. Some perceive the self (soul) as a marvel, some talk of it as a marvel, and some hear of it as a marvel; but even after hearing of it, no one truly knows it.

2.30. O Arjuna, the self (soul) that dwells within the body of every being can never be killed. So you should not grieve for any being.

2.31. In view of your own duty (as a warrior), you must not waver, since there is nothing greater for a warrior than a battle of righteous duty.

2.32. O Arjuna, warriors are fortunate when such a battle comes to them, for it is an open door to heaven.

2.33. But if you do not engage in this battle of righteous duty, you will neglect your own duty and your honor, thereby incurring sin.

2.34. People will always tell of your disgrace, and for a noble person, shame is worse than death.

2.35. Great warriors will think that you retreated from battle due to fear. Those who have high regard for you will disrespect you.

2.36. Your enemies will ridicule you with unkind words and belittle your ability. What could be more worrying than that?

2.37. O Arjuna, if you are killed in this battle, you will gain heaven. If you are triumphant, you shall enjoy the earth. Therefore, stand up with determination to fight.

2.38. Be alike in joy and sorrow, gain and loss, victory and defeat, and be prepared for battle. By doing so, you shall incur no sin.

2.39. (So far) what has been explained to you is the wisdom of Sankhya (philosophy); now hear about the wisdom of yoga (spiritual discipline). O Arjuna, with this wisdom you will break from the bondage of karma (action).

2.40. No effort on this path is lost and there is no harm; even a little practice of this righteousness can save one from great fear.

2.41. With those following this path, the resolute understanding is one-pointed, O Arjuna, but the (wandering) thoughts of those who are irresolute are many-branched and without end.

2.42-43. Those who are unwise and full of desires, whose aim is to reach heaven and who declare that there is nothing else, take delight in the Vedas (Vedic scriptures) and utter flowery words, performing many ritual acts aimed at attaining enjoyment and power, but this only offers rebirth as the fruit of actions.

2.44. For those who are attached to pleasure and power, and whose minds are swept away by such (flowery words), no resolute understanding is found in concentration.

2.45. O Arjuna, the scriptures (Vedas) tell us about the three gunas (qualities of nature — ignorance, passion and goodness). Arise beyond these three qualities, be free from all dualities (e.g. joy and sorrow), be forever fixed in goodness, from acquiring and keeping, and remain self-possessed.

2.46. As much use as a well has in a place where everywhere is flooded, so are the Vedas of use to a learned Brahmin (priest).

2.47. You have a right to action (work), but never to its fruits. Seeking the fruits of action should never be your motive, but never be attached to inactivity.

2.48. O Arjuna, be fixed in yoga (mental discipline): perform actions, relinquish attachment, and stay even-minded in success and failure. This evenness of mind is called yoga.

2.49. O Arjuna, (selfish) action is inferior by far to the yoga of (the discipline of) intelligence. Therefore, seek refuge in intelligence. Those who seek the fruits (of their actions) are miserable.

2.50. One whose intelligence is disciplined renounces (the results of) both good and evil actions in this world. So, strive for yoga. Yoga is skill in action.

2.51. The wise, with disciplined intelligence, having given up the fruits born of action, are released from the bondage of rebirth, and reach the state that is free from misery.

2.52. When your intelligence crosses beyond the cloudiness of delusion, then you will become indifferent to all you have heard (in the Veda), and all that is yet to be heard.

2.53. When your intelligence, which is bewildered by the scriptures (Vedas), stands steady, unshakable in concentration, then you will attain yoga.

2.54. **Arjuna said:** O Krishna, what is a person like, whose wisdom is steady and who is firmly set in concentration? How does one speak? How does one sit? How does one walk?

2.55. **The Lord said:** O Arjuna, when one surrenders all desires of the mind and is satisfied with the self within oneself, that person is said to be one whose wisdom is steady.

2.56. One whose mind is not disturbed in misfortune, who does not crave for pleasures, and whose passion, fear, and anger have vanished, such a person is called a stable-minded sage.

2.57. One who is unattached to all, and who neither rejoices nor hates whether one encounters good or bad, that person's wisdom is deemed stable.

2.58. When one fully withdraws one's senses from their objects, like a tortoise retracting its limbs, that person's wisdom is stable.

2.59. Sense objects (enjoyments) fade away from the embodied self when one abstains from them, but the taste for them stays on; but even the taste disappears when the Supreme is realized.

2.60. O Arjuna, even when a wise person strives (for self-control), the wavering senses forcibly carry away the mind.

2.61. Having restrained all the senses, one should sit focused on Me, for when the senses are under control one's wisdom is stable.

2.62. When one dwells on sense objects, attachment to them grows; from attachment comes desire, and from desire anger arises.

2.63. From anger confusion arises, from confusion comes loss of memory, from loss of memory understanding is lost, and when understanding is gone, one is ruined.

2.64. But one who engages sense objects with the senses controlled and is without likes and dislikes, such a self-controlled person attains serenity.

2.65. In tranquility all of one's sorrows no longer exist, for the understanding of a person whose mind is peaceful is soon established.

2.66. For a person without discipline there is no understanding, nor is there concentration. Without concentration one has no peace, and without peace, how could there be happiness?

2.67. When the mind gives way to the wandering senses, they carry away one's intelligence just as the wind carries away a boat on the water.

2.68. Therefore, O Arjuna, when one's senses are fully withdrawn from their objects, one's intelligence is steady.

2.69. When it is night for all beings, one who is self-controlled is awake; and when beings are awake, it is night for the sage who sees.

2.70. Just like waters entering the ocean, which is always being filled without being disturbed, so is one into whom all desires enter but who is not disturbed attains peace, but not the one who is full of desires.

2.71. One who renounces all (selfish) desires, and who moves (acts) free from cravings and without the notion of "I" or "mine," that person attains peace.

2.72. O Arjuna, this is the divine state; having achieved it, one is free from delusion. One who is established in it, even at the moment of death, attains the nirvana (bliss) of Brahman.

CHAPTER 3

The Path of Action

3.1. **Arjuna said:** O Krishna, If you think that knowledge is better than (the path of) action, then why do you engage me in this terrible act (of war)?

3.2. You are confusing me with words that seem conflicting. So tell me definitely the way by which I may attain what is good.

3.3. **The Lord said:** O Arjuna, in the past I taught two (spiritual) paths in this world — the path of knowledge (jnana yoga) for sankhyas (the followers of wisdom), and the path of selfless action (karma yoga) for yogis.

3.4. A person cannot attain freedom from action by merely abstaining from action, nor could one attain perfection just by renunciation.

3.5. No one can remain inactive even for a moment. All beings, even if they are unwilling, are driven to act by the gunas (the qualities) born of prakriti (material nature).

3.6. One who restrains one's organs of action (hands, feet, tongue etc.), but keeps allowing one's mind to dwell on the objects of the senses, that person is deluded and is said to be a hypocrite.

3.7. O Arjuna, but one who controls the senses with the mind and engages one's organs of action in the yoga of selfless action (karma yoga) without attachment, that person excels.

3.8. So perform your necessary duties, since action is better than inaction. Without action it is not possible even to maintain your own body.

3.9. This world is bound by (the results of) actions, unless it is done for the sake of sacrifice (yajna). So Arjuna, perform your actions without attachment.

3.10. When living beings in ancient times were created along with sacrifice, the Lord of Beings said, "By sacrifice you shall bring forth. Let this be your wish-fulfiller cow, bringing all you desire."

3.11. Honor the gods with sacrifice, and they will honor you. By honoring one another you will attain the highest good.

3.12. Honored by sacrifice, the gods will fulfill your desires. One who enjoys their gifts without offering to them in return is a thief.

3.13. Devotees who eat the remains of (food offered in) sacrifice (yajna) are freed of all sins, but selfish people, who cook only for themselves, eat sin.

3.14. From food creatures come forth, food comes from rain, from sacrifice comes rain, and sacrifice comes from (performing) action.

3.15. Action originates from Brahman (the Vedas), and the Vedas arise from the Imperishable; hence, the all-pervading Brahman is ever present in sacrifice.

3.16. O Arjuna, one who does not follow here (in the world) this cycle thus set in motion is sinful; delighting in sensual pleasures, that person lives in vain.

3.17. But for one who finds joy in the self alone, who is pleased and is content in the self, there is no more work to be done.

3.18. For that person there is nothing to gain in this world by actions done or not done, nor does that person depend on other beings.

3.19. So, without attachment, always perform your duties. By performing (selfless) actions without attachment, one attains the Supreme.

3.20. King Janaka and others achieved perfection by action alone. Therefore, with the view to sustain the world, you must act.

3.21. Whatever a great person does, others will (try to) follow. Whatever standard that person sets, people follow the same.

3.22. O Arjuna, in the three worlds (upper, middle, and lower regions) there is nothing that has to be performed by Me, nor is there anything unattained that has to be attained, yet I continue to engage in action.

3.23-24. O Arjuna, if I did not engage untiringly in action, then people everywhere would follow My way (example). These worlds would perish if I ceased to perform action, and I would be the cause of disorder and the destruction of these beings.

3.25. Just as the unwise perform actions with attachment, O Arjuna, so should the wise perform actions, but without attachment, desiring to sustain the world.

3.26. The wise must not unsettle the minds of the unintelligent who are attached to action. Performing actions with discipline, the wise should encourage them in all their activities.

3.27. All actions are carried out by the qualities of material nature. But one who is deluded by self-centeredness thinks that, "I am the doer."

3.28. O Arjuna, one who understands the real essence of the division of nature's qualities and their actions knows that it is the qualities (gunas) which are acting on qualities, and does not get attached.

3.29. Those who are bewildered by the gunas of prakriti (qualities of material nature) get attached to the actions of the gunas (the qualities). The wise who know the whole should not agitate the dull-witted who have lesser knowledge.

3.30. Offer all actions to Me. With your mind set on the supreme Self, and free from desire and selfishness, fight without sorrow, O Arjuna!

3.31-32. Those who always follow My teachings with faith, and do not complain, gain freedom from the bondage of actions. But those who find fault, and do not follow My teachings, such unintelligent people who are deluded in all knowledge are lost.

3.33. Even those who are wise act according to their own nature. All living beings follow their nature. What can restraint do?

3.34 Attraction and hatred for sense objects are rooted in the senses. One should not fall under the rule of these two, for they are one's enemies.

3.35. It is better to perform **one's own duty (dharma)**, though not perfectly done, than someone else's duty well. It is better to die performing one's own duty, for someone else's duty is unsafe.

3.36. **Arjuna said:** O Krishna, what drives a person to commit sinful acts, even against one's own will, as though compelled by force?

3.37. **The Lord said:** It is desire and anger, which arise from nature's quality of passion (rajas). Know this to be the devouring and sinful enemy here (on earth).

3.38. Just as fire is obscured by smoke, as a mirror by dust, as an embryo is covered by the womb, so is (knowledge) obscured by that (selfish desire).

3.39. O Arjuna, knowledge is obscured by this constant enemy of the wise in the form of desire, an unquenchable fire.

3.40. It has been said that the senses, the mind, and the intellect are its seat. By means of these, desire clouds knowledge and bewilders the embodied self.

3.41. Therefore, O Arjuna, first control your senses, then kill this evil that destroys knowledge and discernment.

3.42. The senses are said to be great, the mind (manas) is greater than the senses, the intellect (buddhi) is greater than the mind, and greater yet than the intellect is the self.

3.43. O Arjuna, knowing that the self is superior to the intellect, control the (lower) self by the (higher) self, and kill the enemy in the form of desire, which is so difficult to overcome.

CHAPTER 4

The Path of Knowledge

4.1. **The Lord said:** I taught this imperishable yoga to Vivasvat (sun god). Vivasvat told it to (his son) Manu (progenitor of humankind) and Manu told it to (his son) Ikshvaku.

4.2. O Arjuna, noble sages knew this yoga, which was passed on in succession, but over the course of time it was lost (forgotten).

4.3. Today, I declare to you the same ancient yoga, a profound secret, because you are My devotee and My friend.

4.4. **Arjuna said:** Your birth is recent, but Vivasvat was born a very long time ago. How can I understand that You declared this (to Vivasvat) in the beginning?

4.5. **The Lord said:** O Arjuna, both you and I have passed through numerous births. I know all of them, but you do not know them.

4.6. Though I am unborn, imperishable, and the Lord of all beings, keeping control of My own material nature, I manifest Myself through My own maya (mysterious power).

4.7. O Arjuna, whenever dharma (righteousness) decays and disorder rises, then I manifest Myself.

4.8. I come into being from age to age to protect the righteous and to destroy the evildoers, so as to re-establish righteousness.

4.9. O Arjuna, one who really understands My divine birth (manifestations) and actions is not reborn upon leaving the (physical) body, that person comes to Me.

4.10. Freed from passion, fear and anger, fully engrossed in Me, and taking shelter in Me, many purified by the fire (austerity) of knowledge have attained to My state of being.

4.11. Whatever way people seek shelter in Me, I accept them. O Arjuna, people follow My path in all ways.

4.12. Those wanting success from their actions on earth sacrifice to the gods; for in this world of humans, they get success from such actions quickly.

4.13. I created the four classes of society according to the division of gunas (the qualities of nature) and karma (action). Though I am the creator of this, know Me to be the eternal non-doer.

4.14. I have no desire for the fruits of action, and actions do not taint Me. One who understands this about Me is not bound by actions.

4.15. Knowing this, the ancient seekers of liberation performed actions. Therefore, you should perform actions as the ancients (seers) did in the past.

4.16. What is action and what is inaction? Even the wise are baffled about this. I shall explain to you what action is, and by understanding that, you will be freed from evil.

4.17. The way of action is difficult to comprehend. One should understand action, what the wrong action is, and what inaction is.

4.18. One who sees action in inaction, and inaction in action, is wise among people. Such a person is disciplined in doing all actions.

4.19. One whose endeavors are free from desire and selfish intentions, and whose actions have been burnt up (made pure) by the fire of knowledge, the wise say, such a person is learned.

4.20. One who has relinquished all attachment to the fruits of action, and who is always satisfied and independent, that person does nothing at all, even if engaged in action.

4.21. One who has no desires, whose mind and self are restrained, who has renounced all (cravings for) possessions, that person, performing actions with the body only, incurs no sin.

4.22. One who is pleased with what comes by chance, who has crossed beyond the pairs of opposites (e.g. joy and sorrow), who is free from envy, and who is even-minded in success and failure, such a person even when acting is not bound.

4.23. The action of a person who is unattached, whose mind is firmly fixed in knowledge and who does work as sacrifice is totally dissolved.

4.24. Brahman is the offering, the oblation is Brahman; it is offered by Brahman into the (ritual) fire of Brahman. Brahman is to be attained by contemplating on the action as Brahman.

4.25. Some yogis (those of discipline) offer sacrifice (in worship) to the gods, while others sacrifice with offerings into the fire of Brahman.

4.26. Others offer their senses (hearing etc.) as sacrifice into the fires of restraint, and others offer sound and other objects of the senses into the fires of the senses.

4.27. Others offer all the activities of the senses and the actions of vital breath (prana) into the fire of the yoga of self-control, kindled by knowledge.

4.28. Others who keep strict vows offer their material possessions, their austerities, their yogic practices, or their study of the scriptures (Vedas) and their knowledge.

4.29. Others who practice breath control, regulate the flow of vital breaths, and offer exhaled breath into the incoming breath and inhaled breath into the exhaled breath.

4.30. Others, limiting their food, offer vital breaths into vital breaths. All these understand what sacrifice is, and by sacrifice their sins are destroyed.

4.31. Those who eat the remnants of sacrifice attain the eternal Brahman. O Arjuna, this world is not for one who does not sacrifice, so how could the other world be?

4.32. Many forms of sacrifice have been spread out in the mouth of Brahman (in the Vedas), and they are all born of action. Knowing this you shall be liberated.

4.33. The sacrifice of knowledge is greater than sacrifice with material things. O Arjuna, all actions, without exception, conclude in knowledge.

4.34. Acquire this knowledge by humility, by questioning, and by your service. Those who are wise and who perceive the truth will impart knowledge to you.

4.35. Having gained this knowledge, you will never be confused again. O Arjuna, by this knowledge you will see all beings within yourself and also in Me.

4.36. Even if you are the worst of all sinners, you shall cross over all sin by the boat of knowledge.

4.37. Just as a burning fire turns wood into ashes, O Arjuna, so the fire of knowledge reduces all actions to ashes.

4.38. On this earth there is no purifier like knowledge. One who is perfected in yoga will over time discover this in oneself.

4.39. A person of faith, who is dedicated to knowledge and whose senses are controlled, gains knowledge, and having achieved it, such a person quickly attains the highest peace.

4.40. But an unwise person, who has no faith and who is filled with doubt, is lost. For one who doubts there is no joy, neither in this world nor the next.

4.41. O Arjuna, one who has renounced (the fruits of) actions through yoga, who has dispelled doubts with knowledge, and who is self-possessed, is not bound by actions.

4.42. Therefore, cut the doubt in your heart that arises from ignorance with the sword of knowledge. O Arjuna! Turn to yoga! Arise!

CHAPTER 5

The Renunciation of Action

5.1. **Arjuna said:** O Krishna, You praise renunciation of actions, and then again you praise (karma) yoga. Now tell me for sure which of the two is better.

5.2. **The Lord said:** Both renunciation of action and the performance of selfless actions (karma yoga) lead to supreme bliss. However, of the two, selfless action is better than renunciation (sannyasa) of actions.

5.3. O Arjuna, a true renouncer is one who neither hates nor desires; free from dualities (e.g. likes and dislikes), such a person is easily freed from bondage.

5.4. The unintelligent say sankhya (the path of wisdom) and (karma) yoga (the path of selfless action) are different, but the wise do not. A person who is very established in one of these gets the reward of both.

5.5. The goal achieved by the sankhyas (followers of wisdom) is also achieved by yogis (followers of yoga). One who sees sankhya and yoga as one, really sees.

5.6. O Arjuna, renunciation is hard to achieve without yoga. However, a sage disciplined in yoga quickly reaches Brahman.

5.7. One who is disciplined, who is pure (in heart), who has controlled the self and senses, and who sees oneself as one with the self of all beings, that person even when engaged in action is not tainted.

5.8-9. Such a disciplined person, knowing the truth, thinks, "I do nothing at all," whether seeing, hearing, touching, smelling, eating, walking, sleeping, breathing, talking, excreting, grasping, or opening or closing the eyes. That person thinks that it is only the senses that are engaged with sense objects.

5.10. One who has given up attachment and devotes all actions to Brahman is untouched by evil, as a lotus leaf is untouched by water.

5.11. For self-purification, yogis (those of discipline) perform actions with their body, mind, intellect, and even with their senses, without attachment.

5.12. By renouncing the fruits of action, one who is disciplined attains lasting peace. But one who is not disciplined, being driven by desire, is attached to the fruits and therefore bound (by selfish actions).

5.13. Having mentally surrendered all actions, the embodied self resides calmly in its city of nine gates (the body, having two eyes, two ears, two nostrils, the mouth, the anus, and the reproductive organ), neither doing anything nor causing action.

5.14. The Lord creates neither agency, nor actions, nor the connection of actions with their fruit. It is nature that does this.

5.15. The all-pervading Lord does not take on anyone's good or evil deeds. Knowledge is obscured by ignorance, hence beings are deluded.

5.16. But for those whose ignorance has been destroyed by knowledge of the self, knowledge illuminates the Supreme like the sun.

5.17. Those with their thoughts, self, and their goal set on That, and who are fully devoted to That (the Supreme), they get cleansed of all sins by knowledge, and reach that state from which there is no return (no rebirth).

5.18. The wise see with an equal eye a l earned and respected Brahmin (priest), a cow, an elephant, a dog, and even an outcaste.

5.19. Even here in this world, creation (birth and death) is overcome by those whose minds are firm in equality. Brahman is perfect and impartial, hence, they are established in Brahman.

5.20. One should not rejoice upon getting what is pleasant, nor become agitated when getting what is unpleasant. Free from delusion, and firm in understanding, that knower of Brahman abides in Brahman.

5.21. One whose self is unattached to outside contacts (sense objects) will find joy in the self (within). United by yoga to Brahman, one attains eternal bliss.

5.22. The enjoyments that arise from sense contacts are sources of sorrow. O Arjuna, they have a beginning and an end. A wise person takes no delight in them.

5.23. One who is able to withstand here in this world, before one is freed from the body, the force arising from desire and anger is a disciplined and joyful person.

5.24. One who finds joy within, light within, and whose happiness is within, such a disciplined person attains to the (heavenly) bliss of Brahman.

5.25. Those sages whose sins have been destroyed, whose doubts have been driven out, who are self-disciplined, and who take joy in the good of all beings, they attain to the (heavenly) bliss of Brahman.

5.26. For ascetics who are free from anger and desire, whose thoughts are controlled, and who know the self, the blissfulness of Brahman is near.

5.27-28. Having locked out external (sense) contacts, focusing the gaze between the eyebrows, keeping the flow of inward and outward breaths within the nostrils in harmony; the sage whose senses, mind, and intellect are controlled, who is intent on liberation, and who is free from desire, anger and fear, attains everlasting freedom.

5.29. One who knows Me as the recipient of all sacrifices and austerities, and as the great God of all worlds and the friend of all beings, such a person attains peace.

CHAPTER 6

Self-discipline

6.1. **The Lord said:** One who performs action that ought to be done with no dependence on the fruits of action is a renouncer (sannyasi) and a yogi; not one who renounces the ritual fire and does not perform any rites.

6.2. O Arjuna, what they call renunciation (sannyasa), know that as yoga. No one becomes a yogi who has not given up selfish intentions.

6.3. For one who aims to rise to yoga, (selfless) action is the means, and for one who has ascended to yoga, tranquility is declared to be the means.

6.4. When one no longer clings to objects of the senses and to actions, and has given up all (selfish) intentions, then that person is said to have attained yoga.

6.5. One should uplift oneself by the self, not degrade oneself, for one's own self is one's friend and one's enemy.

6.6. The self is a friend of one who has conquered one's (lower) self by the (higher) self, but for one who has not conquered one's self, the self gets hostile like an enemy.

6.7. The higher self of one who has conquered one's (lower) self and is tranquil stays poised in heat and cold, in joy and sorrow, and in honor and dishonor.

6.8. The yogi who is contented with knowledge and understanding, who stays unchanged and has control over the senses, and to whom a piece of clay, a stone, and gold are the same, is said to be disciplined.

6.9. A person is remarkable when even-minded towards friends, allies, enemies, neutrals, mediators, relatives, hateful people, the virtuous and even sinners.

6.10. A yogi (practitioner of yoga or a person of discipline) should dwell in a secluded place alone, with the self and mind under control, free from desires and (the craving for) possessions, and constantly concentrate on the self.

6.11-12. (For the practice of yoga), set a seat in a pure (clean) place, neither too high nor too low, covered with grass, a deerskin, and cloth. On that seat, with the mind one-pointed, and restraining the activities of the mind and senses, the yogi should practice yoga for self-purification.

6.13-14. Keeping the body, head, and neck upright and steady, the yogi should gaze at the tip of the nose without glancing elsewhere. Peaceful, free from fear, firm in a vow of chastity, and with the mind restrained and all thoughts on Me, the yogi should sit engrossed in Me.

6.15. By constant discipline, the yogi with the mind restrained attains peace, the highest bliss that is in Me.

6.16. O Arjuna, yoga is not for one who eats too much nor too little, nor is it for one who sleeps too much, nor for one who stays awake too long.

6.17. Yoga (mental discipline) ends all distress for one who is regulated in eating and recreation, in sleeping and waking, and in performing actions.

6.18. When one's controlled thought is set on the self alone, then that person with all longings gone is said to be disciplined.

6.19. Just like a lamp which does not flicker in a place where there is no wind, that is the comparison for the yogi whose thought is restrained and practicing yoga (self-discipline).

6.20. When one's thought comes to rest, controlled by the practice of yoga, one finds fulfillment in the Self, seeing the Self by way of the self.

6.21-22. When one knows that utmost joy, which is grasped by the intellect and is beyond the senses; that in which established, one does not deviate from the truth; when attaining it one thinks there is no other gain greater, and when established there, one is not disturbed even by great sorrow.

6.23. That state is known as yoga — severing one's union with sorrow. One should practice yoga with great determination, and with a steadfast mind.

6.24. Completely relinquish all desires born of selfish intent, and control the senses on all sides with the mind.

6.25. One should gradually come to rest, with one's intelligence held firm, and focusing the mind on the self and not thinking of anything else.

6.26. Wherever one's restless and wavering mind wanders, one should restrain it and bring it back under the self's control.

6.27. A yogi whose mind is at peace, whose passions are under control, and who is without sin, attains the highest joy and becomes one with the Supreme (Brahman).

6.28. Thus, constantly disciplining the self, the yogi free from sin easily achieves the highest bliss of oneness with Brahman.

6.29. One who is disciplined by yoga sees one's self in all beings, and all beings in one's self. Such a person sees the same in all.

6.30. One who beholds Me everywhere, and sees everything in Me, for that person I am never lost, nor is that person lost for Me.

6.31. One who is established in oneness with Me, and who worships Me as present in all beings, regardless of how one exists, that person lives in Me.

6.32. One who, by comparing oneself with others, sees the same in all, whether it be joy or sorrow, O Arjuna, I consider that person to be the highest yogi.

6.33. **Arjuna said:** O Krishna, this yoga of even-mindedness You have declared, I do not see the firm basis of it due to restlessness (of mind).

6.34. O Krishna, because the mind is unsteady, turbulent, adamant and powerful, I believe that to restrain it is as difficult as restraining the wind.

6.35. **The Lord said:** Without doubt, O Arjuna, the mind is restless and difficult to control, but constant practice and non-attachment can restrain it.

6.36. In My opinion, yoga is hard to achieve by one without self-control, but for a person who is self-controlled it can be achieved if one strives by the appropriate means.

6.37. **Arjuna said:** O Krishna, What happens to a person who has faith but lack control due to one's mind straying away from yoga, thereby not achieving perfection in yoga?

6.38. O Krishna, does such a person not perish like a torn cloud, fallen from both, unsteady and bewildered on the path of Brahman?

6.39. O Krishna, you must get rid of my doubt completely, for no one else but You can remove this doubt.

6.40. **The Lord said:** O Arjuna, one is neither doomed in this world, nor in the next. One who does good deeds, My friend, never meets an evil end.

6.41-42. One who has fallen from yoga (yogic discipline) reaches (heavenly) worlds of those who had done good deeds, dwelling there for a great number of years, until one is reborn in the home of a good and prosperous family, or one is born in a family of yogis who are full of wisdom. But such a birth in this world is very rare.

6.43. There one regains the wisdom of one's previous birth and then strives again for perfection, O Arjuna.

6.44. By that previous practice one is carried helplessly forward. Even one who seeks to know yoga goes beyond what is set forth in the Vedas.

6.45. Thus striving with determination, a yogi who has been cleansed of all sins, and is perfected after many births, attains the highest goal.

6.46. A yogi is greater than an ascetic, and also greater than the wise (sage) and the doers of (ritual) action, so become a yogi, O Arjuna.

6.47. Of all yogis, one who is faithful and adores Me, and whose inner self is engrossed in Me, I regard that yogi as the most disciplined.

CHAPTER 7

Knowledge and Insight

7.1. **The Lord said:** O Arjuna, hear how with your mind attached to Me, and practicing yoga with dependence on Me, you can know Me fully and without doubt.

7.2. I will fully explain to you this knowledge along with discernment. By knowing this, there is nothing more left to be known in this world.

7.3. Out of thousands of people, maybe one strives for perfection; and among those who strive and succeed, rarely one knows Me in truth.

7.4-6. My material nature is eightfold: earth, water, fire, air, ether, mind, ego and intellect. This is My lower nature. O Arjuna, know My higher nature, the life-principle by which this world is maintained. Know that all beings arise from these two natures. I am the source of the whole world, as well as its dissolution.

7.7. O Arjuna, nothing is higher than Me. Everything (that exists) is strung on Me, like pearls upon a string.

7.8. O Arjuna, I am the taste in the waters, the light in the moon and the sun, the sacred syllable Om in all the Vedas, the sound in ether, and the valor in men.

7.9. I am the pure fragrance in the earth, the brilliance in fire, the life in all beings, and the austerity in ascetics.

7.10. O Arjuna, know Me as the eternal seed of all beings, the intelligence of the intelligent, and the splendor of the splendid.

7.11. I am the strength of the strong, without passion and desire. O Arjuna, in all beings I am the desire (kama) that is not contrary to righteousness (dharma).

7.12. Know that whatever beings are of sattva (goodness), rajas (passion) and tamas (ignorance or darkness) comes from Me. They are in Me, but I am not in them.

7.13. Bewildered by these states of the three gunas (qualities of nature), this whole world fails to know Me, the Imperishable, transcending them.

7.14. My divine maya (illusory power) comprised of the gunas (nature's qualities) is hard to overcome, but those who take refuge in Me alone overcome this (illusion).

7.15. Those confused sinners who are the lowest of humankind do not take refuge in Me. Their knowledge has been carried away by maya (illusion), and they are of demonic nature.

7.16-18. O Arjuna, there are four types of virtuous people who worship Me: those who are in distress, the seekers of knowledge, the seekers of wealth, and the wise. Of these, a wise person who is always disciplined and whose devotion is single-minded, surpasses them all. I am very dear to such a person and that person is dear to Me. All these devotees are good, but I consider the one who is wise as My very self, for such a person, who is self-disciplined, sees Me alone as the highest goal.

7.19. It is after numerous births that a person of wisdom comes to Me, thinking that "Vasudeva (Krishna) is all." Such a great soul is very hard to find.

7.20. But those whose knowledge is swept away by numerous desires turn to other gods, observing many rites, driven by their own nature.

7.21. Whatever form (deity) any devotee chooses to worship with faith, I will make that person's faith steady.

7.22. With such faith, a person seeks that deity's favor and obtains their desires, but they are only granted by Me.

7.23. The rewards for those with little intelligence are limited. Those worshippers of gods go to the gods, but those who worship Me, come to Me.

7.24. Those who are unintelligent think that I, the Unmanifest, have come into manifestation. Such people do not know My higher nature, which is imperishable and supreme.

7.25. Veiled by My yoga-maya (yogic power of illusion), I am not manifest (visible) to all. This deluded world fails to recognize Me as birthless and imperishable.

7.26. O Arjuna, I know all beings, those of the past, the present, and those yet to come, but no one knows Me.

7.27. O Arjuna, from birth, all beings become bewildered by the delusion of the pairs of opposites, arising from desire and hatred.

7.28. But people of virtuous deeds, whose sins have ended, and who are released from the bewilderment of the pairs of opposites (e.g. joy and sorrow), they worship Me with firm vows.

7.29. Those who strive to be freed from old age and death, and who have taken shelter in Me, they know Brahman, the self, and all action (karma).

7.30. Those who know Me with regard to beings, the divine, and the foremost sacrifice, those with their minds disciplined, know Me even at the time of death.

CHAPTER 8

The Eternal Brahman

8.1. **Arjuna said:** O Krishna, What is Brahman? What is karma? What is adhyatma? What is adhibhuta? And what is adhidaiva?

8.2. O Krishna, what is adhiyajna (the foremost sacrifice), and how is it here within the body? And at the hour of death, how can You be known by those who are self-controlled?

8.3. **The Lord said:** Brahman is the Supreme, the Imperishable. Its essential nature is Adhyatma (the self), and the creative power that brings all beings into existence is called karma (action).

8.4. The adhibhuta is the perishable state, Adhidaiva is the purusha (the spirit), and Adhiyajna (the foremost sacrifice) is Myself abiding in the body, O Arjuna.

8.5. At the time of death, one who remembers Me alone when departing from the body attains to My state, and there is no doubt about this.

8.6. O Arjuna, when leaving the body at the time of death, whatever state of being one remembers, that will one attain.

8.7. Therefore, O Arjuna, always think of Me and fight (do your duty). With your intellect (buddhi) and mind focused on Me, you will definitely come to Me.

8.8. One who is disciplined through the practice of yoga, and who meditates on Me with one's mind not straying elsewhere, that person, O Arjuna, reaches the Supreme Divine Spirit.

8.9-10. At the time of death, one who contemplates on the Ancient, the Ruler, Who is smaller than the smallest, the maintainer of all, of incomprehensible form, and radiant like the sun beyond darkness; that person with a steady mind, with deep devotion, and the power of yoga, focusing the vital breath between the eyebrows, reaches that Supreme Divine Spirit.

8.11. I shall explain to you in short that state which those who are learned in the scriptures (Vedas) call the Imperishable, which ascetics who are devoid of passion enter, and where they follow a life of celibacy.

8.12. Controlling all the (body's) gates, locking the mind in the heart, and holding the vital breath within the head, one is steadfast in concentration through yoga.

8.13. One who, when departing from the body, utters the single syllable Om, which denotes Brahman, and remembers Me, shall reach the highest goal.

8.14. O Arjuna, for a disciplined person who always remembers Me, and whose mind does not stray elsewhere, I am easy to attain.

8.15. Upon reaching Me, those great-souled persons do not go through rebirth, that temporary abode of sorrow, since they have attained the highest perfection.

8.16. O Arjuna, even up to the realm of Brahma (Creator), all worlds are subject to (cycles of) rebirth, but one who has reached Me does not take birth again.

8.17. Those who know that a day of Brahma lasts a thousand ages, and that a night of Brahma ends after a thousand ages, they understand day and night.

8.18. At the coming of day, all beings come out from the unmanifest state, and when night comes all are dissolved into that same unmanifest.

8.19. This multitude of beings that come into being repeatedly are dissolved helplessly when night comes, O Arjuna, and at the dawn of day, they all emerge again.

8.20. But beyond this unmanifest state there is another Unmanifest (existence) that is eternal, and does not perish when all beings die.

8.21. This Unmanifest is called the Imperishable, which is said to be the ultimate goal. Those who reach there do not return (are not reborn). That is My supreme realm.

8.22. O Arjuna, this is the Supreme Spirit to be attained by sole devotion, in whom all beings dwell and by whom all this (universe) is pervaded.

8.23. O Arjuna, now I shall tell you the times when yogis, departing (from this life), return and when they do not return (to this world).

8.24. Those who know Brahman attain to Brahman if they pass away by fire, light, day, in the bright fortnight, or the six months of the sun's northern course.

8.25. But passing away by smoke, night, in the dark fortnight, or the six months of the sun's southern course, the yogi attains the moon's light and returns (is reborn).

8.26. Light and darkness are two eternal pathways of the world. By one, a person does not return; by the other, one returns (is reborn).

8.27. Knowing these two paths a yogi is not bewildered. So stay fixed in yoga at all times, O Arjuna.

8.28. A yogi knowing this goes beyond all the rewards of merit that comes from (studying) the Vedas, from performing sacrifices, austerities, and charities, and attains to the Highest, Primal Abode.

CHAPTER 9

Royal Knowledge and Mystery

9.1. **The Lord said:** I will tell you, who do not complain, the most secret wisdom along with knowledge. Knowing it you will be freed from evil.

9.2. It is sovereign knowledge, a royal secret, supremely purifying, insightful, righteous, easy to practice, and imperishable.

9.3. O Arjuna, those having no faith in this truth do not reach Me; hence, they return to the path of death and rebirth.

9.4. The entire world is pervaded by Me in My unmanifest (hidden) form. All beings exist in Me, but I am not present in them.

9.5. Behold My divine mysterious power; these beings do not exist in Me. Though My Self is the source of all beings and the sustainer of them, yet I do not exist in them.

9.6. Just as the mighty wind, blowing everywhere, always resides within space, so you should know that all beings exist in Me.

9.7. O Arjuna, at the end of every age (cycle) all beings enter into My material nature (prakriti), and at the beginning of a new age, I bring them forth again.

9.8. Through My own material nature (prakriti), again and again I bring forth this multitude of beings, all powerless by the force of nature.

9.9. O Arjuna, these actions do not bind Me for I am unattached to them, seated apart like one who is unconcerned.

9.10. O Arjuna, with Me in control, material nature (prakriti) brings forth living and non-living things, and by this reason the world turns.

9.11. Foolish people disregard Me when I am in a human form. Such people do not know My higher nature, as the great Lord of all beings.

9.12. With their hopes, actions, and knowledge useless, such mindless people abide in a demonic nature that is deceiving.

9.13. O Arjuna, but the great-souled (people) who take refuge in the divine nature, they worship Me with single-minded devotion, knowing that I am the imperishable source of all beings.

9.14. Those who always glorify Me, striving with firm vows, and bowing to Me, they worship Me with devotion, forever disciplined.

9.15. Others, sacrificing with the sacrifice of knowledge, worship Me as the One, as different and as the many, facing everywhere.

9.16. I am the ritual, the sacrifice, the offering (to the ancestors), the healing herb, the sacred hymn, the clarified butter, the (sacred) fire, and I am the oblation.

9.17. I am the father of this universe, the mother, the grandfather, the supporter, the object of knowledge, the purifier, the sacred syllable Om, and the three scriptures (Rig, Yajur, and the Sama Vedas).

9.18. I am the goal, the sustainer, the Lord, the witness, the abode, the refuge, the friend, the source, the dissolution, the basis, the resting place, and the imperishable seed.

9.19. O Arjuna, I give heat, I withhold and I send the rain down. I am immortality, and I am also death. I am both being and non-being.

9.20. Those who are learned in the three Vedas, who drink soma juice (sacrificial offering) and are cleansed of their sins, and worship Me through sacrifices, seeking to attain heaven; they reach the heavenly world of (the Vedic deity) Indra where they enjoy celestial delights.

9.21. After having enjoyed the world of heaven and their merit (of good deeds) has been used up, they return back to this world of mortals. By following the doctrines of three Vedas with desire for enjoyment, what they obtain is temporary (they go and return).

9.22. But devotees who worship Me, and always contemplate steadfastly on Me alone, I bring what they do not have and protect what they have.

9.23-24. O Arjuna, those devotees who worship other gods with deep faith, they are really worshipping Me alone, although it is not the best approach. I am the Lord and the recipient of all sacrifices; however, they do not know My true nature, so they fall (fail).

9.25. Those worshippers of gods go to the gods, those worshippers of ancestors go to the ancestors, those worshippers of spirits go to the spirits, but those who worship Me, come to Me.

9.26. If anyone offers Me a leaf, a flower, a fruit or water with devotion, I will accept that offering from one who has offered it with love.

9.27. O Arjuna, whatever you do, what you eat, what you offer, what you give, and whatever austerities you perform, do all that as an offering to Me.

9.28. Doing so, you shall be freed from the bondage of action (karma), which yields good and evil results. Being disciplined by the yoga of renunciation, you shall be released and will come to Me.

9.29. I am the same to all beings, I neither hate nor favor anyone, but whoever worships Me with devotion, they abide in Me, and I am in them.

9.30. Even if a very evil person turns to Me with sole devotion, that person should be considered good for taking the right resolve.

9.31. In a short time that person becomes righteous and finds everlasting peace. O Arjuna, know that one who is devoted to Me will never perish.

9.32. O Arjuna, those who take shelter in Me, including women, Vaishyas (farmers and traders), and even Shudras (servants), they all attain to the highest goal.

9.33. How much more (easy is it) then for pious priests and royal sages! So while you are in this temporary, unhappy world, devote to Me!

9.34. Focus your mind on Me and be devoted, sacrifice to Me, and bow to Me. Hence, having disciplined your self with Me as your ultimate goal, you shall come to Me.

CHAPTER 10

The Divine Power

10.1. **The Lord said:** O Arjuna, hear again My supreme word, which shall give you joy, and which I will declare for your benefit.

10.2. Neither the multitude of gods know My beginning, nor do the great seers, since in all respects, I am the source of the gods and the great seers.

10.3. One who knows Me to be unborn, without beginning, and the great Lord of the worlds, is undeluded among mortals and is released from all sins.

10.4-5. Understanding, knowledge, non-delusion, forgiveness, truth, self-control, tranquility, joy, sorrow, existence, non-existence, fear, as well as fearlessness, nonviolence, neutrality, contentment, austerity, charity, fame, and ill-fame, are various qualities of beings that arise from Me alone.

10.6. The seven great (olden) seers, the ancient four, and the Manus (progenitors of humankind) were born of My mind. All the beings in this world have descended from them.

10.7. One who (truly) understands My divine glory and power becomes united with Me through unshakable discipline. There is no doubt about this.

10.8. I am the origin of everything, and from Me all comes forth. Understanding this, the wise worship Me with loving devotion.

10.9. Those with their thoughts and their lives devoted to Me, enlightening one another and always talking about Me, they are contented and find delight in Me.

10.10. To those who are ever disciplined, and who lovingly adore Me, I give the yoga (the discipline) of intelligence through which they come to Me.

10.11. Out of compassion for them, I reside in their hearts, and I remove the darkness (within) born of ignorance with the bright light of knowledge.

10.12-13. **Arjuna said:** You are the Supreme Brahman, the Highest Abode, the Ultimate Purifier, the Eternal Divine Spirit, the Primal God, the Unborn, and the All-pervading Lord. So the ancient sages declared about You: the divine sage Narada, as well as Asita, Devala, Vyasa, and now You tell it to me Yourself.

10.14. O Krishna, I believe all You told me to be true. O Lord, neither the gods nor the demons understand Your manifestation.

10.15. O Supreme Spirit, You alone know Yourself by Yourself. You are the Source of beings, the Lord of beings, God of gods, and Lord of the universe.

10.16. Explain to me fully Your divine manifestations through which you pervade these worlds.

10.17. O Lord how could I know You by constantly meditating on You? In what aspects are You to be contemplated on by me, O Krishna?

10.18. O Krishna, tell me in detail of Your divine power and manifestation, for I can never be tired of listening to Your nectar-like (immortal) speech.

10.19. **The Lord said:** O Arjuna, I will now declare to you My divine manifestations, the important ones, for My extent is endless.

10.20. O Arjuna, I am the Self that dwells in the hearts of every being. I am the beginning, the middle, and the end of all beings.

10.21. I am Vishnu among sun gods, among lights I am the radiant sun, among the wind gods I am Marichi, and among the stars I am the moon.

10.22. Among the Vedas (scriptures) I am the Sama Veda, among the gods I am Indra, among the senses I am the mind, and among beings I am consciousness.

10.23. Among the Rudras (storm gods) I am Shiva, among demigods and demons I am Kubera (lord of wealth), among the Vasus I am Agni (god of fire), and among mountains I am Meru.

10.24. O Arjuna, among priests I am the chief Brihaspati, among generals I am Skanda (god of war), and among waters I am the ocean.

10.25. I am Bhrigu among great sages, of words (utterances) I am the single syllable Om, of sacrifices I am the silent prayer (the repetitions), among the immovable I am the Himalayas.

10.26. Among trees, I am the sacred Ashvattha (fig tree), among divine sages I am Narada, among the Gandharvas (celestial musicians) I am Chitraratha, and among the perfected ones I am Kapila the sage.

10.27. Among horses I am the nectar-born Ucchaihshravas, among divine elephants I am Airavata, and among people I am the king.

10.28. Among weapons I am the thunderbolt, among cows I am Kamadhuk (wish-fulfilling cow), of procreating I am Kandarpa (god of love), and among serpents I am Vasuki.

10.29. Among the Nagas (serpents) I am Ananta, among water creatures I am Varuna, among the ancestors I am Aryama, and among controllers I am Yama (lord of the dead).

10.30. Among the Daityas I am Prahlada, among reckoners I am time, among animals I am the lion, and among birds I am Garuda.

10.31. Among purifiers I am the wind, among warriors I am Rama, among water creatures I am the alligator, and among rivers I am the Ganges.

10.32. O Arjuna, of creations I am the beginning, the middle, and also the end. Of knowledge, I am knowledge of the self, and of those who speak I am the discussion.

10.33. Among letters I am the letter "A," and of compounds (in grammar) I am the dvandva (the conjunctive). I am eternal Time and the Creator, facing all sides.

10.34. I am Death, the all-destroying, and the source of all that are yet to come. Of feminine I am fame, fortune, speech, memory, intelligence, steadiness, and patience.

10.35. Of chants I am the Brihat-saman (the great chant), of meters I am the Gayatri, of months I am Margashirsha (Nov. - Dec.), and of seasons I am spring.

10.36. I am the gambling of the deceitful, of the splendid I am the splendor, I am victory, the determination, and I am the goodness of the good.

10.37. Among the Vrishnis I am Vasudeva; I am Arjuna among the Pandavas; among sages I am Vyasa, and I am Ushana among poets.

10.38. I am the rod of rulers, the wise strategy of the seekers of victory, the silence of secrets, and the wisdom of the wise.

10.39. O Arjuna, I am the seed of all beings, there is nothing living or non-living that could exist without Me.

10.40. My divine manifestations are endless. O Arjuna, know what I have told you to be just an example of the extent of My manifestations.

10.41. Whatever has glory, attractiveness and power, know that all have come from a mere fragment of My splendor.

10.42. O Arjuna, of what use is all this knowledge to you? I sustain this entire universe with only a fragment of Myself.

CHAPTER 11

The Divine Universal Form

11.1. **Arjuna said:** Out of compassion, You have told me about the highest mystery of the self, and by this my delusion has been removed.

11.2. O Krishna, I have heard from You in full about the origin and the demise of beings, and about Your everlasting greatness.

11.3. O Lord, I wish to see Your divine form, just as You declared Yourself to be, O Supreme Spirit.

11.4. O Lord, if You think it can be seen, then show me Your imperishable Self, O Lord of Yoga.

11.5. **The Lord said:** O Arjuna, see My forms by hundreds and by the thousands of different colors and shapes.

11.6. O Arjuna, behold the sun gods, the gods of light, the storm gods, the twin gods of sunrise, and the wind gods, so many marvelous forms never seen before.

11.7. O Arjuna, see the whole universe of living and non-living things, and anything else you wish to see, here as one in My body.

11.8. But with your own eyes you cannot see Me, hence, I will give you a divine eye. Now see My divine power!

11.9-14. **Sanjaya** (the reporter) **then said:** O King, after saying this, Krishna, the great Lord of Yoga, then revealed to Arjuna His supremely divine form, having numerous mouths, eyes, celestial ornaments, and with many divine weapons upraised; wearing divine garlands and apparels, anointed with heavenly perfumes, having all wonders, radiant, boundless, and facing all sides. If the light from a thousand suns were to come forth all together in the sky, it might be like the brilliance of that great Spirit. Arjuna saw the whole universe in its diversity, all as one within the body of the God of gods. Arjuna being amazed with what he saw, and with his hairs raised on end, bowed his head to the Lord, and with joined hands (in worship), thus spoke.

11.15. **Arjuna said:** O Lord, I see in Your body all the gods as well as different kinds of beings. I see sages, divine serpents, and Lord Brahma upon hi s lotus throne.

11.16. I see Your endless form on all sides. I see numerous arms, bellies, mouths, and eyes. I see no beginning, nor middle, nor end, O Lord of All, of universal form.

11.17. I behold You with Your crown, with a mace and discus; a mass of light shining all around, having the radiance of blazing fire and the sun on e very side, difficult to see — immeasurable.

11.18. You are the Imperishable Supreme to be known, the supreme refuge of this universe, the protector of eternal law. I regard You as the Primal Spirit.

11.19. I see You with no beginning, nor middle, nor end, of unlimited power, with countless arms, and with the moon and sun as Your eyes. I see Your mouth as a blazing fire, scorching the universe with Your brilliance.

11.20. The entire space between heaven and earth, and in all directions, is filled by You alone. O Great Soul, seeing Your amazing, fearsome form, the three worlds tremble.

11.21. Multitudes of gods enter You. In fear, some with joined hands (in worship) praise You. Crowds of great sages and perfected ones cry out, "Hail!" and praise You with great hymns.

11.22. The Rudras, the Adityas, the Vasus, the Sadhyas, the Vishvedevas, the two Ashvins, the Maruts, the Ushmapas, the Gandharvas, the Yakshas, the Asuras, and Siddhas, all look at You astonished.

11.23. O Krishna, seeing You in Your grand form with numerous mouths, eyes, arms, thighs, feet, bellies and terrible teeth, the worlds tremble, and I also tremble.

11.24. When seeing You (Your form) touching the sky, shining with numerous colors, with Your mouths open and Your large eyes glowing, my innermost self shakes, and I find neither strength nor serenity, O Vishnu (O Lord)!

11.25. Seeing Your mouths with terrible fangs, like the fires of doom, I have lost my sense of direction, and I find no refuge. O Lord of lords, Shelter of the World, be merciful!

11.26-27. Rushing into Your terrible mouths with fearful teeth are the sons of king Dhritarashtra along with hosts of kings, and heroes such as Bhishma, Drona and Karna, as well as our leading warriors. Some of them are even seen with their crushed heads wedged between Your teeth.

11.28. Just as the currents of the rivers rapidly flow towards the ocean, so these heroes of this world enter into Your blazing mouths.

11.29. Just as moths rush swiftly into a blazing fire to their deaths, so these people rush into Your mouths to their doom.

11.30. O Vishnu (O Lord), You devour all the worlds around, licking them up with Your fiery mouths. Your terrible rays fill the whole universe with brilliance and burn it.

11.31. Tell me who You are in this terrifying form. Praise to You, O Supreme Lord, be gracious! I would like to know You, the Primal One, since I do not understand what You do.

11.32. **The Lord said:** I am Time, the destroyer of worlds, coming here to destroy. Even without you, none of these warriors gathered here for battle against you will stay alive.

11.33. So arise and attain glory! Conquer your enemies and enjoy kingship! These warriors have already been killed by Me. You will simply be My instrument, Arjuna!

11.34. Great warriors like Drona, Bhishma, Jayadratha, Karna, and others are already killed by Me. Slay them and do not be worried! Engage in battle and you will overcome your enemies!

11.35. **Sanjaya** (the reporter) **said:** After hearing these words from Krishna, Arjuna, who was trembling, joined his hands in paying homage. In fear, he bowed before Krishna and in a nervous voice, spoke these words.

11.36. **Arjuna said:** O Krishna, The world rightly rejoices and delights in praising You. While crowds of perfected ones bow to You in reverence, frightened demons run away in all directions.

11.37. O Great Lord, and why should they not bow to You (in devotion)? You are the Original Creator, even greater than Brahma. O Infinite One, God of the gods, Shelter of the World, You are the Imperishable; You are being and non-being, and also that beyond both.

11.38. You are the Original God, the Primal Spirit, the Ultimate Refuge of all, the Highest Abode, the Knower and what is to be known. You pervade the entire universe O Lord of Limitless Form!

11.39. You are Vayu (god of the wind), Yama (lord of death), Agni (god of fire), Varuna (god of waters), the moon, the Lord of Beings, and the Great Grandfather. Praise to You, O Lord, a thousand times! Again and again, praise to You!

11.40. Praise to You in front, from behind, and on all sides. O All! of boundless might and immeasurable power. You pervade everything, hence You are all.

11.41-42: Not knowing Your greatness, for whatever I have said rashly, out of negligence or affection, calling You "O Krishna, O Yadava, O friend," and also, if I have displeased You while joking (as in fun), playing, resting, sitting, eating, alone or in company, I beg Your forgiveness, O Immeasurable One.

11.43. You are the Father of the world of the moving and the non-moving. You are its most revered teacher and the object of worship. No one is equal to You, so how could there be anyone in the three worlds greater than You? O Lord of unequaled power!

11.44. So, I bow before You and I ask You to be gracious. O Lord, bear with me as a father to a son, as a friend to a friend, and as a lover to a beloved.

11.45. I am delighted to see what has never been seen before, yet my mind is troubled with fear. O Lord, show me Your other form. Be gracious, O Lord of gods, Shelter of the World.

11.46. I desire to see You as before with Your crown, and with a mace and the discus in Your hands. O Thousand-Armed God of universal form, reveal Your four-armed form.

11.47. **The Lord said:** O Arjuna, by My grace and by My divine power, I have shown you My supreme form — brilliant, universal, infinite, and primeval, which no one but you has ever seen.

11.48. Neither by the Vedas (scriptures), nor by sacrifices, nor by study, nor by charity, nor by rituals, nor by strict austerities can I be seen in this form in the world of mortals by anyone but you, O Arjuna.

11.49. Do not be confused or show fear from seeing this fearful form of Mine. Free from fear, and with your mind composed, now see My familiar form again.

11.50. **Sanjaya** (the reporter) **said:** After saying these words to Arjuna, Krishna revealed His familiar (human) form. The Great One then resumed his gentle form, and calmed the frightened Arjuna.

11.51. **Arjuna said:** O Krishna, seeing Your gentle human form now, my mind is at ease and I have returned to my normal nature.

11.52. **The Lord said:** This (higher) form of Mine that you have seen is very hard to see. Even the divinities are always longing to see this form.

11.53. Neither by the Vedas, nor by austerity, nor by charity, nor by sacrifice, could one see Me in the form that you have seen Me.

11.54. O Arjuna, but solely by devotion, I can be truly known, seen and entered into.

11.55. One who performs work for Me, who sees Me as the Highest Goal, who is devoted to Me, who is without attachment, and who bears no enmity towards anyone, that person comes to Me, O Arjuna.

CHAPTER 12

The Path of Love and Devotion

12.1. **Arjuna said:** Of devotees who worship You ever disciplined, and those who worship the Imperishable Unmanifest (Unrevealed), who has a better understanding of yoga?

12.2. **The Lord said:** I consider those with their minds fixed on Me, and who worship Me with the highest faith and discipline, to be the best in yoga (discipline).

12.3-4. But those who worship the Indestructible, the Indescribable, the Unmanifest, the All-pervading, the Inconceivable, the Eternal, the Unchanging, and the Immovable; and who have controlled all their senses and are even-minded to all, and take joy in the good of all beings, they also attain Me.

12.5. It is harder for those with their minds attached to the Unmanifest, since the goal of the Unmanifest is difficult to attain by embodied beings.

12.6-7. But those surrendering all actions to Me, who are intent on Me, and who meditate on Me with sole discipline, O Arjuna, with their minds set on Me, I soon lift them out of the ocean of death and rebirth.

12.8. So, set your mind on Me alone, let your intellect enter Me, and you will reside in Me hereafter. There is no doubt about this.

12.9. O Arjuna, if you cannot set your thought steadfastly on M e, then strive to reach Me by the steady practice of yoga (concentration).

12.10. Even if you are not capable of practice, then be devoted to work for Me, for by doing this for My sake, you shall attain perfection.

12.11. And even if you are unable to do this, then turn to My yoga, and with self-control, surrender the fruits of all your actions.

12.12. Knowledge is better than practice, better than knowledge is meditation; the renunciation of the fruits of action is better than meditation, for from renunciation peace soon follows.

12.13-14. One who does not hate any being, who is friendly, compassionate, devoid of egoism and possessiveness, the same in joy and sorrow, patient, always contented, self-controlled, resolute, and whose intellect and mind are devoted to Me, such a devotee is dear to Me.

12.15. A person is dear to Me who does not agitate (others in) the world, and who is not agitated by (others in) the world, and who is free from excitement, anger, fear, and anxiety.

12.16. One without expectations, who is pure, capable, uninvolved, unperturbed, and who has renounced all (selfish) undertakings, is dear to Me.

12.17. One who is devoted and neither rejoices nor hates, neither grieves nor craves, and who has relinquished both the favorable and the unfavorable, that person is dear to Me.

12.18-19. One who is the same toward friends and enemies, the same in honor and dishonor, in heat and cold, in joy and sorrow, who is free from attachment, the same in praise and blame, and who is quiet, contented, stable in mind, and not attached to any home, such a devotee is dear to Me.

12.20. Those devotees with faith who follow this nectar of truth as explained by Me, and have Me as their highest goal, they are very dear to Me.

CHAPTER 13

The Field and Its Knower

13.1. **The Lord said:** O Arjuna, this body is called the field, and one who knows it is called the knower of the field. So the wise say.

13.2. Know Me to be the Knower of the field in all fields (bodies). O Arjuna, I consider true knowledge to be knowledge of the field and its knower.

13.3. Now hear from Me in short what the field is, its nature, its changes, whence it arises, and also who the knower is, and what the knower's powers are.

13.4. Sages have sung this in numerous ways, in various hymns, and in convincing and reasoned statements of the sayings about Brahman.

13.5-6. The gross elements (earth, fire, water, air, ether), the intellect, the ego, the unmanifest, the ten senses [seeing, hearing, touching, tasting, smelling, and the five organs of action — mouth (voice), feet, hands, anus, and generative organ] and one (mind), the five objects of the senses (smell, sound, form, touch, and taste), desire, hatred, happiness, pain, the body, consciousness, and resolve. In brief, this is the field along with its changes.

13.7-11. (Knowledge denotes) humbleness, honesty, nonviolence, patience, sincerity, respect for one's (spiritual) teacher, purity, steadfastness, self-control, non-attachment to objects of the senses, absence of selfishness, a perception of the sorrows arising in birth, sickness, old age, suffering and death, detachment, absence of (too much) attachment to children, wife, and home, always being even-minded in favorable and unfavorable situations, unwavering devotion to Me through single-minded discipline, resorting to secluded places, staying away from a crowd of people, steadfastness in knowledge of the self, and perceiving the object of true knowledge. All this is said to be knowledge, and what is contrary to this is ignorance.

13.12. Now I shall explain that which ought to be known, knowing which one attains immortality. It is the Supreme Brahman, beginningless, and said to be neither being nor non-being.

13.13. Its hands and feet are everywhere; with heads, mouths, and eyes everywhere; with ears everywhere. It pervades everything in the world.

13.14. It appears to have the qualities of all the senses, yet devoid of all senses; unattached and yet supporting everything; without the qualities (gunas) and yet experiencing them.

13.15. It is outside and inside of all beings. It is moving and non-moving. It is too subtle to be perceived, and though far away, yet it is near.

13.16. Though it seems divided in all beings, yet it is undivided. It ought to be known as the creator, the sustainer and the absorber of all beings.

13.17. It is the light of all lights and is said to be beyond darkness. It is knowledge, the object, and the goal of knowledge. It resides in the hearts of all beings.

13.18. Thus in brief I have explained the field, as well as knowledge and the object of knowledge. Knowing this, one who is devoted to Me attains to My state.

13.19. Know that prakriti (material nature) and purusha (the spirit or living entity) have no beginning. Know also that the changes and the gunas (qualities of nature) are born of prakriti.

13.20. Prakriti (material nature) is said to be the reason for agency, cause and effects, while the purusha is said to be the cause in experiencing joy and sorrow.

13.21. The living entity (purusha) residing in material nature (prakriti) experiences the qualities (gunas) born of nature (prakriti). Its attachment to the gunas (qualities) is the cause of it being born in good or sinful wombs.

13.22. The Highest Spirit within the body is called the Witness, the Consenter, the Sustainer, the Experiencer, the Great Lord, and the Supreme Self.

13.23. One who knows the living entity (purusha) and material nature (prakriti) with its qualities of nature (gunas) is not born again regardless of how one currently exists.

13.24. Some perceive the self (atman) within themselves by meditation, others by the path of wisdom, and others by the path of selfless actions (karma-yoga).

13.25. Others who do not know this, hear it from other people and worship, hence they also go beyond death by their devotion to what they heard.

13.26. O Arjuna, whatever comes into being, moving or non-moving, know it comes from the union of the field (the body) and its knower (the spirit).

13.27. One who sees the Supreme Lord residing equally in all beings, not perishing when they die, really sees.

13.28. One who perceives the Lord abiding equally everywhere, does not harm the Self by oneself, and thus reaches the highest goal.

13.29. One who perceives that actions are done only by material nature (prakriti), and that the self is the non-doer, that person really sees.

13.30. When one sees the diverse states of being as residing in the One, and expanding from that, then one attains Brahman.

13.31. This imperishable Supreme Self, being beginningless and without qualities (gunas), even though it resides in the body, O Arjuna, it neither acts nor gets tainted (by acts).

13.32. Just as all-pervasive space is not tainted due to its subtlety, so the self dwelling in every body is not tainted.

13.33. O Arjuna, just as one sun illuminates the whole world, so the owner (the self) of the field illuminates the whole field.

13.34. Those who know through the eye of knowledge the difference between the field and the knower of the field, and the liberation of beings from material nature (prakriti), they attain to the Highest.

CHAPTER 14

The Qualities of Nature

14.1. **The Lord said**: I shall again explain to you that supreme knowledge, the highest of all knowledge by which sages have left this world to attain the highest perfection.

14.2. Those turning to this knowledge have attained a nature like Mine. Even at the time of creation they are not reborn, nor troubled at the time of dissolution.

14.3. O Arjuna, the great Brahman (Prakriti/Nature) is My womb; into that I placed the seed, and from that all beings have come forth.

14.4. O Arjuna, of all forms that appear in any wombs, the great Brahman (Prakriti/Nature) is their womb, and I am the Father, the giver of the seed.

14.5. The three gunas (qualities of nature): sattva (goodness or purity), rajas (passion or active desire) and tamas (darkness or ignorance) arise from material nature (prakriti). O Arjuna, they bind the imperishable soul (atman) in the body.

14.6. Sattva (goodness), being pure, is luminous and healthy. O Arjuna, it binds the soul by attachment to happiness and to knowledge.

14.7. Know that rajas, which is of the nature of passion, to be born of longings and attachment. O Arjuna, it binds the embodied soul by attachment to (the fruits of) action.

14.8. Know that tamas, which is born of ignorance, confuses all embodied beings. O Arjuna, it binds (the soul) through negligence, laziness, and (excess) sleep.

14.9. O Arjuna, sattva (goodness) attaches one to joy, and rajas (passion) to action, but tamas (ignorance), concealing knowledge, attaches one to negligence.

14.10. Goodness prevails when it overcomes passion and ignorance. O Arjuna, (at times) passion prevails when it overcomes goodness and ignorance, and (at times) ignorance prevails when it overcomes goodness and passion.

14.11. When the light of knowledge shines in all the gates (senses) in this body, know that goodness has prevailed.

14.12. O Arjuna, when rajas (passion) rises, greed, activity, the undertaking of works, restlessness and cravings arise.

14.13. When tamas (ignorance) rises, O Arjuna, dullness, laziness, negligence and confusion arise.

14.14. If one passes away when sattva (goodness) prevails, the embodied soul enters the pure worlds of the knowers of the Supreme.

14.15. If death happens during the dominance of rajas (passion), one is reborn among those attached to action, and if one dies during the dominance of tamas (ignorance), one is reborn in the wombs of the confused.

14.16. They say that the fruit of good deeds is sattvic and pure, but sorrow is the fruit of rajasic action, and ignorance is the fruit of tamasic action.

14.17. Knowledge arises from sattva, and from rajas greed arises, but from tamas comes confusion, negligence and ignorance.

14.18. Those abiding in sattva go upwards, the rajasic remain in the middle, and the tamasic, the lowest of the gunas, sink lower.

14.19. When a person of vision perceives that there is no other doer but the gunas, and knows That which is beyond the gunas, such a person attains to My being.

14.20. When the embodied self transcends these three qualities (gunas) that are the sources of this body, the self is freed from birth, death, old age, and sorrow, and achieves immortality.

14.21. **Arjuna said:** O Lord, what are the marks of a person who has gone beyond the three qualities (gunas)? How does a person conduct oneself, and how does one cross beyond these three qualities?

14.22. **The Lord said:** O Arjuna, the one who hates neither light, nor activity, nor delusion when they arise, nor craves for them when they no longer exist.

14.23-25. One who sits like one unconcerned, and is not disturbed by the gunas, thinking that only the qualities (gunas) are acting; who stays firm, who is alike in joy and sorrow, who is self-composed, and to whom a lump of earth, a stone, and a piece of gold are alike; who is steady; who is the same in blame and praise, pleasure and displeasure, honor and dishonor, who treats friends and enemies alike, and who has given up all (selfish) undertakings — that person is said to have crossed beyond the qualities (gunas).

14.26. One who serves Me with unwavering love and devotion (bhakti yoga), crossing beyond the qualities of nature, is fit to become one with Brahman.

14.27. For I am the basis of Brahman, of the immortal and imperishable, of the eternal dharma (law), and of perfect bliss.

CHAPTER 15

The Supreme Divine Spirit

15.1. **The Lord said:** It is said that the imperishable Ashvattha tree has its roots above and its branches below. Its leaves are sacred hymns. One who knows this, is a knower of the Vedas (scriptures).

15.2. The branches of this tree spread below and above, and are nourished by the qualities of nature (gunas); its buds are sense objects, and its roots extend downward into the world of humans, tangled with actions.

15.3-4. The (true) form of this tree is not understood here (in this world); neither its beginning, nor its end, nor its foundation. Cut down this solid-rooted tree with the strong axe of detachment. Thereafter, seek to find the abode from which, having reached it, one never returns, (saying); "I take shelter in that Primal Spirit from which ancient activity came forth."

15.5. Those without pride and delusion, who have overcome the faults of attachment, who are absorbed in the self, whose (selfish) desires have ceased, who are freed from the pairs of opposites known as joy and sorrow, they attain that Eternal Abode.

15.6. Neither the sun lights it, nor the moon, nor fire. That is My supreme abode. Reaching it, one does not return (to this world).

15.7. A fragment of Me becomes an eternal (individual) soul in this world of living beings. It attracts to itself the (five) senses and the mind (the sixth) that abides in nature.

15.8-9. When the lord (the self) takes on a body and then departs from that body, it carries these (the mind and senses) along, like the wind carrying scents from their abode; presiding (in another body) over hearing, sight, touch, taste, smell, as well as the mind, it enjoys the objects of the senses.

15.10. Deluded people do not perceive the self when it stays or leaves the body, or experiences sense objects through connection with the gunas, but those with the eye of knowledge are able to see.

15.11. Yogis who strive (through yoga) see the self within themselves, but those who are unwise and without self-control, even though striving, fail to see.

15.12. That brilliance in the sun, which illuminates the whole world, and that which is in the moon and in fire, know that brilliance to be Mine.

15.13. I enter the earth, and with My power I support all beings, and becoming Soma (moon), I nourish all plants.

15.14. Becoming the digestive fire (of life) within the bodies of all beings, and uniting with vital breaths (in and out), I digest the four kinds of food.

15.15. I dwell in the hearts of everyone, and memory, wisdom and reasoning arise from Me. I a m to be known by all the scriptures (Vedas), and I am the knower of the Vedas and the author of Vedanta (doctrine).

15.16. In this world there are two Purushas (spirits), the perishable and the imperishable. All beings (bodies) are perishable, but the imperishable is called the unchanging.

15.17. But other than these two is the highest Spirit called the Supreme Self, the eternal Lord, Who enters the three worlds and maintains them.

15.18. Because I am beyond the perishable, and higher than the imperishable, I am well-known in the world and in the Vedas as the Supreme Spirit (Purushottama).

15.19. Whoever is undeluded and knows Me as the Supreme Spirit (Purushottama), knows it all. O Arjuna, such a person worships Me with their whole being.

15.20. Thus I have taught you the most secret doctrine, O Arjuna; understanding it, one becomes (truly) wise, and one's purpose (in this life) is accomplished.

CHAPTER 16

Divine and Demonic Attributes

16.1-3. **The Lord said:** These are the qualities of those born with the divine nature: fearlessness, pureness of heart, perseverance in the yoga of knowledge, charity, self-control, sacrifice, study of the scriptures, austerity, uprightness, nonviolence, truthfulness, absence of anger, renunciation, peace, absence of slander, compassion for all beings, absence of greed, kindness, modesty, steadiness, vigor, forgiveness, resolve, purity, absence of malice and absence of too much pride.

16.4. O Arjuna, the qualities of those born with the demonic nature are: deceitfulness, arrogance, pride, anger, harshness, and ignorance.

16.5. It is said that the divine qualities lead to freedom, while the demonic qualities lead to bondage. O Arjuna, do not worry, for you are born with divine qualities.

16.6. In this world there are two kinds of created beings, the divine and the demonic. The divine was explained to you in depth; now hear from Me, O Arjuna, about the demonic.

16.7. Demonic people do not know what is to be done and what should not be done. They have no purity, no good conduct, and no truth in them.

16.8. They claim that the world has no truth, no (moral) foundation, no law of creation, that it is without God, and that it is caused by (lustful) desire.

16.9. Clinging to these views, such lost souls with poor intelligence and of terrible deeds arise as enemies of the world, seeking to destroy it.

16.10. Attached to insatiable desire, full of pride, hypocrisy and arrogance, as well as having false notions due to delusion, they work with impure intentions.

16.11. Overwhelmed with innumerable anxieties that end only with death, their highest aim is to satisfy their desires, believing that this is all.

16.12-15. Bound by a hundred chains of expectations, gripped with anger and lust, they gather wealth by unfair means to satisfy their cravings. (Some say) "I have gained this today; and I shall get that too; this wealth is my own, and I will gain more. I've killed this enemy, and I shall kill others as well. I am the lord, I enjoy, I am a successful person, powerful and happy. I am wealthy, and I am of high rank. Who is equal to me? I shall perform sacrifice, I shall give (alms), and I shall rejoice." This is what people who are deluded by ignorance say.

16.16. Confused by numerous thoughts, tangled in the net of delusion, and attached to the gratification of desires, they fall into a polluted hell.

16.17. Self-centered, obstinate, and drunk with the pride of wealth, they perform sacrifices (yajnas) only in name (for show), and without following (scriptural) rules.

16.18. Driven by self-centeredness, power, pride, lust, and anger, these envious people hate Me in their own bodies, as well as in others.

16.19. These cruel and sinful people, the lowest of humankind, I hurl them down repeatedly into demonic wombs through cycles of birth and death.

16.20. Entering into demonic wombs, these confused people, in life after life, fail to attain Me, hence they sink to the lowest state, O Arjuna.

16.21. The three gates to hell that lead to self-ruin are desire, anger, and greed; therefore, one must give up these three.

16.22. O Arjuna, one who is set free from these three gates of darkness, does what is good for one's self, and then reaches the Highest Goal.

16.23. But one who rejects the teachings of scriptures and follows one's own (selfish) desires, finds neither perfection, nor happiness, nor the highest goal.

16.24. Therefore, let the scriptures be your guide in determining what you ought to do and what you ought not to do. Understanding what is prescribed by the scriptures, perform actions here (in this world).

CHAPTER 17

The Three Kinds of Faith

17.1. **Arjuna said:** O Krishna, What is the nature of those who ignore the rules of the scriptures, yet worship with full faith? Is it sattva (goodness), rajas (passion), or tamas (ignorance)?

17.2. **The Lord said:** The faith of the embodied (being), born of one's own nature, is of three kinds: sattvic, rajasic or tamasic. Now hear from Me about this.

17.3. O Arjuna, the faith of each person is according to their nature. A person is made of faith, and whatever one's faith is, so that person is.

17.4. Sattvic people worship the gods, the rajasic worship demigods and demons, and tamasic people worship ghosts and spirits.

17.5-6. Those who perform severe austerities that are not in keeping with the scriptures, who are full of hypocrisy and conceit, and who are driven by the force of desire and passion, they torture the elements that constitute their bodies and also Me dwelling in them; know the resolves of such foolish people to be demonic.

17.7. Food that is dear to people is of three kinds, and so too are sacrifice, austerity and charity. Now listen to their distinctions.

17.8. Foods that are dear to people of sattva are tasty, nourishing, wholesome, and satisfying. They increase life, energy, strength, health, and joyfulness.

17.9. Foods that are dear to people of rajas are bitter, sour, salty, hot, pungent, dry, and burning. They cause distress, pain, and sickness.

17.10. Foods that are dear to people of tamas are tasteless, stale, spoiled, unclean, and leftover.

17.11. Sacrifice that is performed in keeping with the scriptures by those not craving for any reward, and who (honestly) believe that it should be done, is said to be sattvic.

17.12. But sacrifice that is done in hope of a reward and for the sake of show, O Arjuna, know that to be rajasic.

17.13. Sacrifice that is not in keeping with the scriptures, and which is done without the offering of food, without sacred hymns, without faith, and without gifts (to the priest) is considered tamasic.

17.14. Austerity of the body consists of honoring the divinities, priests, teachers, and the wise; also cleanliness, uprightness, chastity and nonviolence.

17.15. Austerity of speech is speaking words that are not offensive, which are truthful, helpful, and pleasing, as well as reciting the scriptures.

17.16. Austerity of the mind consists of calmness of mind, kindness, silence, self-control, and purity within.

17.17. This threefold (mind, speech and body) austerity, when practiced with the highest faith by those who are disciplined and who do not crave for reward, is said to be sattvic.

17.18. Austerity which is done for the sake of gaining respect, praise, reverence, and done only for show is said to be rajasic. It is unsteady and temporary.

17.19. Austerity which is performed with silly ideas, with torturing oneself, or with the aim to harm others, is said to be tamasic.

17.20. Charity (gift) when given without the expectation of anything in return, and (with the feeling) that it is a person's duty to give to a worthy person at a suitable place and time, is said to be sattvic.

17.21. But charity when given with the expectation of a service (or gift) in return or in hope of gaining a reward or when given grudgingly is said to be rajasic.

17.22. Charity given at an unsuitable place and time to an unworthy person, and offered disrespectfully and with contempt, is said to be tamasic.

17.23. Om Tat Sat is declared as the threefold designation of Brahman, and by this, the Brahmanas, the Vedas, and the sacrifices were ordained in olden times.

17.24. Therefore, knowers (devotees) of Brahman always begin acts of sacrifice, charity, and austerity as prescribed in the scriptures by uttering Om.

17.25. Those who seek liberation utter Tat in acts of sacrifice, charity, and austerity without desire for any reward.

17.26. Sat denotes what is good and true. O Arjuna, it is also used to denote good deeds that are worthy of praise.

17.27. Resoluteness in sacrifice, austerity and charity is also called Sat, and any action associated with these is also known as Sat.

17.28. But whatever offering, charity given, and austerity that is done without faith is called Asat. O Arjuna, it is useless here (in this world) and hereafter.

CHAPTER 18

Liberation by Renunciation

18.1. **Arjuna said:** O Lord, I wish to know the real essence of renunciation (sannyasa) and of relinquishment (tyaga), and how they are different.

18.2. **The Lord said:** Sages understand renunciation as the giving up of actions arising from desire; but the surrender of the fruits of all actions is what the wise declare as relinquishment.

18.3. Some who are wise say that action is tainted and should be relinquished, but others declare that acts of sacrifice, charity, and austerity should not be relinquished.

18.4. O Arjuna, now hear My decision about relinquishment. Relinquishment is said to be of three kinds.

18.5. Acts of sacrifice, charity and austerity should be performed, not relinquished, for these acts purify those who are wise.

18.6. These actions should be performed without attachment to them and their rewards. O Arjuna, this is My definite view.

18.7. It is not proper to renounce prescribed work. The relinquishing of work (one's duty) due to delusion is declared to be of the nature of tamas.

18.8. Those who relinquish their work (duty) because it is difficult, or from fear of bodily distress, their relinquishment is considered rajasic, hence they do not get the reward of relinquishment.

18.9. But one who does prescribed work because it should be done, relinquishing attachment and the reward, O Arjuna, that relinquishment is said to be sattvic.

18.10. Such a wise relinquisher whose doubts have been dispelled, and who is full of goodness, neither dislikes unpleasant work, nor gets attached to pleasant work.

18.11. It is not possible for any embodied being (person) to relinquish actions completely; but one who surrenders the rewards of action is called a relinquisher (tyagi).

18.12. The fruits of action for those who have not relinquished them, when they die, are threefold: desired, undesired, and mixed. But for the renouncer there is none.

18.13-15. O Arjuna, hear from Me the five factors for the accomplishment of all actions as declared in Sankhya (doctrine). They are the body, the doer, the various instruments (senses), the various kinds of activities, and lastly, fate as the fifth. Whatever action one performs with one's body, mind, or speech, whether it is good or bad, these are the five factors.

18.16. This being so, one who considers oneself to be the only doer, because of one's poor intelligence, is foolish and does not see (clearly).

18.17. But one who is free from selfishness and whose intelligence is not tainted, even if one slays these people, one does not kill them and is not bound (by this action).

18.18. Knowledge, the object of knowledge, and the knower — these are the threefold urgers of action. The action, the doer, and the instrument are the three constituents of action.

18.19. Knowledge, action, and the doer are declared in the theory of gunas to be of three kinds, according to their qualities (gunas). Now hear about them from Me.

18.20. Knowledge by which one perceives one imperishable existence in all beings, undivided in the divided, know that knowledge as sattvic.

18.21. Knowledge by which one perceives many existences of different kinds, as separate in all beings, know that knowledge to be rajasic.

18.22. But knowledge by which one is attached to one thing as if it were the whole, and which is trivial, devoid of reason, and lacking truth, that knowledge is said to be tamasic.

18.23. Action that is necessary and which is done without attachment, and without desire or hatred by one who does not crave for its fruit, is said to be sattvic.

18.24. Action that is performed with much effort by one seeking to satisfy one's desires, or done out of selfishness, is said to be rajasic.

18.25. But action done under delusion, without any concern to consequences, loss, harm, or to one's own ability, is said to be tamasic.

18.26. A doer who is without attachment and is not conceited, who is steadfast and persevering, and who is unbothered by success or failure, is said to be sattvic.

18.27. A doer who is passionate, who craves for the fruits of action, who is greedy, violent (in temperament), impure, and who is moved by joy and grief, is said to be rajasic.

18.28. A doer is said to be tamasic, who is undisciplined, uncultured, stubborn, cunning, dishonest, lazy, dejected, and procrastinating.

18.29. O Arjuna, hear about the threefold division of understanding and determination, explained in detail and separately according to nature's qualities (gunas).

18.30. O Arjuna, one who understands when to act and when not to act, what should be done and what is not to be done, what to fear and what is not to be feared, and what bondage and freedom are, that understanding is said to be sattvic.

18.31. O Arjuna, one who cannot distinguish between what is right and what is wrong, and what should be done and what is not to be done, that understanding is rajasic.

18.32. That understanding which, concealed by darkness, considers what is wrong to be right, and sees everything to be distorted, is tamasic, O Arjuna.

18.33. That determination by which one restrains the activities of the mind, the vital breaths and the senses by steadfast yoga is sattvic, O Arjuna.

18.34. O Arjuna, that determination by which one clings to duty, to pleasure and wealth with attachment and craving for the fruits, is rajasic.

18.35. That determination by which one who is unintelligent cannot give up fear, grief, dejection, pride, and (excess) sleep is tamasic, O Arjuna.

18.36. O Arjuna, hear from Me about the three kinds of happiness, wherein one finds delight by long practice, and reaches the end of sorrow.

18.37. This joy which seems like poison initially but in the end is like nectar, and which arises from the calmness of one's own mind, is said to be sattvic.

18.38. That joy which comes from contact of the senses with their objects, and which seems like nectar initially but is like poison in the end, is said to be rajasic.

18.39. That joy which arises from sleep, laziness, and negligence, and which deludes the self both initially and in the end, is said to be tamasic.

18.40. There is no being on this earth or among the divinities in heaven, who is free from these three qualities (gunas), born of material nature (prakriti).

18.41. The actions (duties) of the Brahmins (priests), the Kshatriyas (warriors and leaders), the Vaishyas (farmers and merchants), and the Shudras (servants) are differentiated according to the qualities (gunas) born of their own nature.

18.42. Serenity, self-control, austerity, purity, forgiveness, uprightness, knowledge, insight, and faith (in the Lord) are actions of the Brahmins (priests) born of their nature.

18.43. Heroism, vigor, resolve, skill, bravery in battle, generosity, and leadership are actions of the Kshatriyas, born of their nature.

18.44. Farming, cattle-herding and trade are actions of the Vaishyas, born of their nature, while the actions of the Shudras consist of works of service.

18.45. Each person attains perfection by performing their own work (duty). Hear how one who is devoted to one's own duty attains perfection.

18.46. One attains perfection by worshipping the Lord, Who is the source of all beings, and by Whom all this (universe) is pervaded, through one's own action (duty).

18.47. It is better to perform one's own duty even though it is not perfectly done than to do a nother person's duty well. By performing action (work) ordained by one's own nature, one avoids sin.

18.48. O Arjuna, a person should not relinquish the work one is born to (that is natural to one), even if it is imperfect, for all undertakings are clouded with imperfections, just as fire is clouded by smoke.

18.49. One whose intelligence is unattached to everything, who is self-controlled and free from desire, attains through renunciation the highest perfection of freedom from action.

18.50. Hear from me in short, O Arjuna, how one who has reached perfection attains to Brahman, the highest state of knowledge.

18.51-53. With purified intelligence, having restrained oneself with resolve, relinquishing sound and other objects of the senses, free from attraction and hatred, dwelling in a secluded place, eating less, controlling the mind, speech and body, always absorbed in the yoga of meditation (dhyana yoga), taking shelter in dispassion; having renounced egoism, violence, arrogance, desire, anger, and possessiveness; unselfish and calm, one is fit to be one with Brahman.

18.54. Being one with Brahman, at peace in the self, one neither grieves nor desires. Equal-minded to all beings, one achieves the highest devotion to Me.

18.55. Through devotion one comes to know Me, about My extent and Who I really am; then knowing Me in truth, one enters into Me instantly.

18.56. By constantly performing all actions, and taking shelter in Me, one attains the eternal, imperishable abode by My grace.

18.57. Mentally surrender all actions to Me, be intent on Me, resort to the yoga of (the discipline of) intelligence, and focus your thoughts always on Me.

18.58. By setting your thoughts on Me, you shall overcome all obstacles by My grace. If, however, due to egoism you do not hear Me, then you shall perish.

18.59. Your resolve will be useless if out of egoism you say, "I will not fight." Nature will force you to (act).

18.60. O Arjuna, what you do not want to do, due to your delusion, you shall do even if you are unwilling, since you are bound by your own karma (action) born of your nature.

18.61. O Arjuna, the Lord resides in the hearts of every being, making all revolve by the Lord's Maya (mysterious power), as though they are mounted upon a machine.

18.62. O Arjuna, go to the Lord alone for refuge with your whole being, and by the Lord's grace, you shall attain supreme peace and the everlasting abode.

18.63. This knowledge I have declared to you is the most secret of all. Reflect fully on it, then do as you wish.

18.64. Hear once more My supreme word, the deepest secret of all. Because you are dear to Me, I will speak for your benefit.

18.65. Let your mind be fixed on Me, worship Me, sacrifice to Me, adore Me, and you will come to Me, I truly promise you, because you are dear to Me.

18.66. Relinquish all duties and take shelter in Me alone. Do not worry, for I shall release you from all sins.

18.67. Never tell this (knowledge) to one who does not practice austerity, nor to one who is without devotion, nor to one who does not wish to hear it, nor to one who resents Me.

18.68-69. One who shares this supreme secret with My devotees and gives Me the highest devotion, shall surely come to Me. No one among people does greater service to Me than that person, nor will there be anyone on earth dearer to Me than that person.

18.70. And in My view that person who shall study our dialogue, by that one I shall be worshipped through the sacrifice of knowledge.

18.71. Even one who listens to it with faith and without envy shall be freed, and attain to the blissful worlds of the virtuous.

18.72. O Arjuna, have you listened (to these teachings) with full attention? Has your delusion born of ignorance been removed?

18.73. **Arjuna said:** O Krishna, my delusion has disappeared and by Your grace my memory is regained. I now stand firm, free from doubt, and ready to act according to Your word.

18.74. **Sanjaya** (the reporter) **said:** And so I heard this remarkable conversation between Lord Krishna and the great-souled Arjuna.

18.75. By the grace of the sage Vyasa, I heard this supreme secret, yoga, directly from Krishna Himself, the Lord of Yoga.

18.76. O King, when remembering this wonderful and sacred dialogue between Lord Krishna and Arjuna, again and again I rejoice.

18.77. When recalling again and again, that wondrous form of Hari (Vishnu, Krishna), O King, I am greatly amazed, and I rejoice over and over again.

18.78. Wherever Krishna, the Lord of Yoga is, and wherever there is the archer Arjuna, I believe there will be fortune, victory, prosperity, and righteousness.

Jagdish R. Singh (Roy) is the author of a number of fiction and non-fiction titles including *Strange Misfortunes, Adventures of the Homeless, The True Self, The Tolerance of Hinduism, Days of Laughter,* as well as a collection of essays titled *Earthly Tribulations,* and fourteen fictional stories under the title *Pandora's Heartaches.* Having studied spiritual beliefs and ancient myths, he has been actively writing fiction and non-fiction themes that are thoughtful and informative.

www.ingramcontent.com/pod-product-compliance
Lightning Source LLC
Chambersburg PA
CBHW071302040426
42444CB00009B/1835